CROSSROADS OF THE WORLD

Recollections From An Airport Town

CROSSROADS OF THE WORLD

Recollections From An Airport Town

Roderick B. Goff

Flanker Press Ltd.
St. John's, NL
2005

Library and Archives Canada Cataloguing in Publication

Goff, Roderick B., 1916-
Crossroads of the world : recollections from an airport town / Roderick B. Goff.

ISBN 1-894463-86-2

1. Goff, Roderick B., 1916- 2. Gander (N.L.)--History--20th century.
I. Title.

FC2199.G34G64 2005 971.8 C2005-906714-4

PRINTED IN CANADA

FLANKER PRESS
ST. JOHN'S, NL, CANADA
TOLL FREE: 1-866-739-4420
WWW.FLANKERPRESS.COM

Canada

Canada Council for the Arts Conseil des Arts du Canada

We acknowledge the financial support of: the Government of Canada through the Book Publishing Industry Development Program (BPIDP); the Canada Council for the Arts which last year invested $20.3 million in writing and publishing throughout Canada; the Government of Newfoundland and Labrador, Department of Tourism, Culture and Recreation; the Newfoundland and Labrador Arts Council.

Contents

Foreword

The flight of the seven Hudsons has been given special attention in this book because, in the opinion of the author who witnessed the takeoffs from Gander, it was a pivotal flight in the conquest of the North Atlantic by aircraft under winter conditions.

The technical information that was gained by the subsequent thousands of delivery flights to the United Kingdom in wartime was of inestimal value in the development of commercial aviation over the North Atlantic in the postwar years.

This book was written in Gander; the manuscripts were typed by Marilyn Puddicombe.

All stories in this book are covered by a copyright issued in Ottawa, Ontario in 2005.

Roderick B. Goff
September 30, 2005

The publisher would like to thank Kelly Vincent for recommending it to Mr. Goff.

To the memory of my wife, Alice

Gander: The Evolution of An Airport Town

IN JUNE 1936, WHEN A GROUP of fifty workers disembarked from the train at Milepost 213, along the then trans-insular Newfoundland railway, they were employed to start clearing the bush for the construction of an airport.

The high plateau, 500 feet above sea level, had been selected earlier as an ideal location for a world-class airport. Nearby, majestic Gander Lake was seen as suitable for the operation of flying boats.

By December 1938, the airport was ready to receive aircraft. At that time, meteorological staff, radio operators, and other employees moved to Gander from Botwood, which had been the refuelling stop for the flying boats of Imperial Airways, Pan American Airways, and American Export Airlines.

The first aircraft to operate successfully across the North Atlantic from the new airport was piloted by Captain Donald C.T. Bennett. His aviation experience included service in the

Royal Australian Air Force (RAAF), the Royal Air Force (RAF), and as captain of the Imperial Airways flying boats on the North Atlantic route.

Leading a group of seven Hudson bombers that were being delivered to the RAF, he took off from Gander at 10:30 p.m. Greenwich Mean Time, November 10, 1940 and arrived at Aldergrove, Ireland at 9:40 a.m. on November 11. The pilots of the six Hudsons following Bennett were equally successful.

The flight of the seven Hudsons was pivotal in establishing the feasibility of flying aircraft over the North Atlantic in winter conditions. Subsequently, thousands of various types of military aircraft operating through Gander over the North Atlantic provided technical knowledge to aircraft manufacturers and commercial airlines. As a result, commercial air traffic from Gander started almost immediately after the Second World War ended in August 1945.

CROSSROADS OF THE WORLD

As air travel increased in the postwar period, airlines grew in number and offered travellers a variety of routes and schedules.

Air travel was soon available, not only from New York, but also from Chicago, Detroit, Toronto, Montreal, Boston, and Halifax to places such as Shannon, London, Prestwick, Amsterdam, Paris, Frankfurt, and Rome. In that exciting period of aviation, when airlines used propeller-driven aircraft, intercontinental air travel between North America and Europe required a refuelling stop at Gander. Within a short time, Gander would become known as "the crossroads of the world."

In order to handle the thousands of transatlantic passengers passing through Gander and to provide essential service for the hundreds of aircraft, Hangars 21 and 22 – formerly used by the RAF Ferry Command – were taken over by the airlines. Once alterations were made, the spacious passenger lounge in Hangar 22, with an adjoining dining room and Big Dipper bar, was believed to be the largest airport lounge in North America.

Hangar 21 housed the meteorological office, flight dispatch offices, and aircraft maintenance shops. When air travellers had to spend the night at Gander, they were accommodated in three former RAF Ferry Command buildings: Jupiter; Saturn; and Mars.

Employment opportunities with airlines and government services attracted hundreds of young people to Gander, and many had valuable war-time experience to offer. Many civilians who had worked during the war also had skills that proved attractive in the new era of aviation.

With the sudden influx of people, suitable accommodation had to be provided to single and married people. Within a short time, scores of former military barracks were converted into comfortable apartments and single rooms. A former U.S. Air Force sergeants' mess was made into a spacious dining room with adjoining lounge, club facilities, and bar. This building, frequently the setting for impromptu parties, was soon dubbed "The Airlines Hotel."

By the end of 1950, there were more than 3,000 people living at the airport. Churches, schools, a movie theatre, and a library were established in former military buildings. The owners of the first business in Gander, Goodyear-Humber Stores, needed a larger building, and a few other businesses became part of the community.

The radio broadcasting station operated by the RCAF was taken over by the Newfoundland Broadcasting Company, and the huge RCAF recreation building was turned into an ice rink, named Gander Gardens.

The RCAF Banting Memorial Hospital was taken over by the Newfoundland Department of Health in 1946. It provided medical service to residents of Gander and nearby settlements. On April 1, 1946, Dr. James Paton was the single doctor on duty and Alice Goff, RN was the only professional nurse on duty.

When Newfoundland became a province of Canada in April 1949, Ottawa's Department of Transport assumed control and management of Gander. It soon became evident that, due to the deterioration of the former military buildings and the growing population, there was a need for a townsite. A site approximately three miles from the airport was selected.

The first fifty houses were completed on the townsite in 1952. All houses were rental units, twenty-six of which were prefabricated structures imported from England. By the end of 1953, 100 rental units had been completed for Department of Transport employees.

Meanwhile, Gander residents who were veterans of the Second World War had been granted a special area for the construction of their homes. The first home completed in the area, Beaverwood, is still owned by the family of its builder, the late Edgar Baird, a former RAF flight lieutenant pilot.

The pace of home construction increased considerably when fully-serviced building lots were offered for as low as $350 per lot. By 1955, more than 200 of the town's 327 houses were privately owned. As well, forty-five lots were sold to businesses, and plans were made to build two supermarkets, a movie theatre, and a bank. Five churches and two schools soon went under construction.

On January 1, 1955, a municipal government was established by order of the Lieutenant-Governor-in-Council. A board of trustees was appointed to administer the town. The first town manager was Eli Baker, a former high-school teacher.

In 1956, the Canadian Broadcasting Corporation (CBC) opened a new building in the town. As well, a new airport terminal was constructed on the south side of the airport and formally opened by Queen Elizabeth II in June 1959. By 1961, a hospital was under construction along the Trans-Canada Highway: today's James Paton Memorial Hospital.

On January 8, 1959, the town of Gander attained full status as a municipality when residents elected their first mayor and six councillors. All served without remuneration. The first mayor, the late Jack Robertson, had been one of the first group of radio operators stationed in Botwood during the era of the flying boats, and had served with the RCAF during the Second World War.

TECHNOLOGY BRINGS CHANGE

When long-range jet aircraft were introduced to intercontinental travel in 1959, there was a gradual decrease in the number of refuelling stops made at Gander.

By 1961, while the major airlines were using long-range jets, smaller carriers and charter flights continued to use propeller-driven aircraft. Also, the Gander-based airline, Eastern Provincial Airways expanded to add a schedule airline within the province, with original routes serving St. John's, Gander, Deer Lake, Stephenville, Goose Bay, the power-development centres of Twin Falls and Churchill Falls, and the mining town of Labrador City–Wabush.

In 1963, EPA purchased Maritime Central Airways and formed a new company, Eastern Provincial Airlines (EPA), with headquarters in Gander. The routes of the new company were extended to include Montreal and Toronto.

The expansion of EPA gave a financial boost to the town of Gander. In 1983, EPA, controlled by local businessman Harry Steele, was purchased by Canadian Pacific Airlines (CP Air), which later became part of Canadian Airlines.

The success of the revolution in Cuba, led by Fidel Castro, also had a positive effect on Gander. After three years of fighting, Castro seized power in 1959. His Communist government and his subsequent alliance with the U.S.S.R. resulted in an airline service between Havana and Moscow, with refuelling stops at Gander. Duty time limitations meant Cuban and Russian crews often took rest periods in Gander, and they were made to feel welcome in the town. This service continued for more than thirty years.

However, in 1992, because hundreds of refugees were using Gander as an entrance to Canada, the Department of Citizenship and Immigration established a Canadian visa requirement for all passengers on Aeroflot and Cubana aircraft when refuelling stops were made at Gander. As a result, these airlines tended to avoid Gander and refuel at other airports, such as Shannon, Ireland.

When both Aeroflot and Cubana advanced to using long-range JFT aircraft on the Moscow–Havana route, refuelling stops at Gander were only rarely an operational requirement. While the use of long-range jet aircraft had a negative effect on the number of landings at Gander Airport, numerous executive aircraft, charter flights, and military aircraft continued to use the facilities of the airport on their North Atlantic flights.

The national airline – Air Canada – is represented in Gander and offers connecting flights to mainland airports and to Air Canada Trans-Atlantic flights from St. John's. Air Labrador and Provincial Airlines Limited (PAL) also serve Gander. Other aviation activities at Gander include a flying school, a Canadian Armed Forces Search and Rescue Unit, and an Air Traffic Control Centre. A factory which produces plastic component parts for the new Cormorant helicopters of the Canadian Armed Forces was opened in 1999 and is located near the Search and Rescue Unit.

The high plateau which was seen originally as an ideal location for a world-class airport also lends itself as an ideal location for the modern, well-planned town that ultimately grew to its present population of approximately 10,000 people. Because one can walk around the many streets, avenues, crescents, and the business areas of Gander without encountering a steep hill, it is an ideal retirement town for seniors.

Since the completion of the Trans-Canada Highway in 1965 and the subsequent construction of a paved highway connecting Gander to such places as Gander Bay, Carmanville,

Musgrave Harbour, Wesleyville, and Gambo, Gander has become an important shopping centre in the central part of the island of Newfoundland. A sports-minded town, Gander offers facilities for softball, soccer, tennis, golf, badminton, swimming, and the winter sports of hockey, curling, skating, and skiing. For residents who are interested in the arts and other cultural activities, there is a well-stocked town library, and membership is always open in the Avion Players drama group and the Centre Chorale singing club. Each year, the Arts and Culture Centre is the venue for a spring music festival and a summer music camp for schoolchildren. The club rooms of the fraternal societies, the Golf Club and the Canadian Legion Club, are settings for social events, including games of bingo and darts.

The schools in Gander, and the Gander branch of the College of North Atlantic, have always maintained a high standard of scholarship. This standard of excellence is reflected in the army of Gander's baby boomers who have moved on to become skilled aircraft mechanics, long-range jet aircraft pilots, teachers, lawyers, doctors, engineers, nurses, architects, research scientists, air traffic controllers, and politicians of Cabinet rank. Some have spread their wings to other parts of Canada and the U.S.A. while others chose to reside in Newfoundland and Labrador.

The town of Gander may be seen to have entered the new millenium with pride, grace, and dignity on May 5, 2000. On that date, the town's new seven-million-dollar Community Centre was opened by Mayor Claude Elliott. The fifty workers who started to clear the bush at Milepost 213 in June 1936 would have been pleased.

THE FLIGHT OF THE SEVEN HUDSONS

ON NOVEMBER 10, 1940, SEVEN Lockheed Hudson bombers departed from Gander Airport in what was considered to be, at that time, a daring operation which would prove that it was indeed feasible to deliver badly needed bombers to the United Kingdom by air. The delivery of bombers by air was not only more expeditious than by sea but also would involve the lesser risk, in view of the reality that the sea routes of the North Atlantic were infested with German sub-

Shown above are the aircrew members who operated the flight of the seven Hudsons from Gander Airport on November 10, 1940. The Newfoundland Railway car in the background is one of three railway cars that provided accommodation for the airmen during their stopover in Gander. Donald C.T. Bennett, who led the historic flight, is shown standing bare-headed at the far right. (Photo by Griffith Powell, Department of National Defence, Canada, DND/CF Photo, PMR 85/475)

marines. Therefore, the flight of the seven Hudsons was an important, pivotal flight.

Preparing weather maps for the airmen of the RAF Ferry Command at the Gander weather office. L-R: G. Lester; J. Moakler; R.B. Goff.

The Hudson bombers were manufactured by the Lockheed Aircraft Company in Burbank, California, and went into production in September 1940. Only two months later, seven of these aircraft were on a Gander Airport runway, poised for takeoff on the first bomber delivery flight over the North Atlantic.

The Hudson was a twin-engine aircraft, the approximate dimensions of which were a wingspan of twenty metres, a length of fifteen metres, and a height of four metres. The normal operating crew of the Hudson for the ferry operation was a pilot, navigator, and a radio operator.

From California, the Hudsons were flown to St. Hubert Airport in Montreal, where special training for the ferry operator was given to the airmen who were selected from the many volunteers. The key person in the entire operation, from the time the Hudsons departed from California until they arrived in the United Kingdom, was an Australian, Donald Clifford Tyndall Bennett.

Although Captain Bennett had only reached his thirtieth birthday on September 14, 1940, he had already established a distinguished peacetime record in aviation. He had served in both the Royal Australian Air Force and the Royal Air Force. He had flown the North Atlantic as captain of the flying boats of Imperial Airways. In 1938, he established a world long-distance record for seaplanes when he piloted one from Scotland to South Africa. It is evident why, as a superb pilot and navigator, Captain Bennett was selected to direct and lead the flight of the seven Hudsons.

In due time, after Captain Bennett had checked out all the aircrew and the performance of each Hudson, the seven aircraft were flown to Gander Airport by that elite group of airmen who would deliver the seven Hudsons to the United Kingdom.

Because there were limited accommodations at Gander Airport at that time, the airmen were accommodated in three railway cars that were on loan from the Newfoundland Railway Company. During their few days at Gander awaiting suitable flying weather, two of the railway cars were used for sleeping quarters while the third car was their dining room.

Prior to the flight of the seven Hudsons, the airmen proceeded to the Gander office of the Meteorological Service of Canada (MSC), where they were briefed by the then manager, Patrick Duncan McTaggart-Cowan, a native of British Columbia. As a Rhodes Scholar, he had acquired a reputation as a hard-working, dedicated, and reliable forecaster of North

Atlantic weather when he was stationed at Botwood in the 1930s. At that time, Botwood was used by Imperial Airways, Pan American Airways, and American Export Airlines as a refuelling stop on the North Atlantic commercial passenger service.

In fine professional style, and with an obvious high degree of confidence, McTaggart-Cown advised the airmen where they would probably encounter turbulent air, precipitation, and icing conditions. After answering a series of relevant questions from the airmen, he presented each captain with a weather folder which gave a graphic description of the overall en route weather. A glance at the opened folder showed the height of both the base and the tops of clouds, the temperatures, as well as the direction and speed of winds at various altitudes along the planned route. The weather folder also included forecasts for the weather at the destination airport, Aldergrove, Ireland, and for alternate airports in the United Kingdom that could be used in the event that Aldergrove airport was not operational at landing time.

The actual departures of the seven Hudsons from Gander Airport were made in a very colourful setting. The regimental band of Queen's Own Rifles of the Canadian Army positioned themselves near Hangar 20, from which the Hudsons were taxied to the takeoff runway. While the band played lively martial music and a small group of civilians and military people watched in awe and admiration, Captain Bennett made the first takeoff at 2233 Greenwich Mean Time. In time intervals of approximately two minutes, he was followed by the six other Hudsons, respectively in the command of

Captains Adams, Andrews, Cripps, Lyons, Rogers, and Smith. Among the twenty-two airmen who operated the flight of the seven Hudsons that night, there were nine Americans, six British, six Canadians, and one Australian.

RAF Ferry Command Hudsons parked at Hangar 20, Gander Airport, Nevember 10, 1940, prior to takeoff for United Kingdom.

Within the limits of wartime secrecy and the negative effects of en route weather, radio communications were maintained within the group during the flight and with radio operators who were stationed at ground stations on both sides of the North Atlantic. While the pilots flew the Hudsons and peered into the dark November night with frequent glances at their instruments, the navigators were busy establishing their respective positions as they progressed toward their destination. At the same time, the radio operators aboard the Hudsons maintained two-way communication with the radio operators at Gander Airport and with their counterparts in Ireland and the United Kingdom.

Weather information was sent to each Hudson in an encoded digital form which could be decoded by the aircrew who carried in their flight documents the key to all weather codes. The original plan to fly the seven Hudsons in close formation for the entire flight was abandoned at about mid-distance, when hazardous weather was encountered in the form of heavy turbulence, snow, and icing conditions. By breaking formation, not only was the possibility of aircraft collision avoided, but also each captain was free to deal with the difficult weather at his own discretion, by changing his flight altitude or by otherwise modifying the original flight plan.

Captain Bennett landed his Hudson safely at Aldergrove at 0945 Greenwich Mean Time, eleven hours and twelve minutes after he had taken off from Gander Airport. By so doing, he had earned the distinction of delivering safely to the United Kingdom the first bomber via the North Atlantic air route.

In due time, he was followed by the six other captains, who were equally successful in landing at Aldergrove without incident. It was then November 11, the twenty-second anniversary of the signing of the armistice that officially ended the First World War of 1914–1918.

The flight of the seven Hudsons, which began with a colourful takeoff ceremony, terminated with a splash of colour of a different nature. Captain Bennett carried with him a supply of Remembrance Day poppies. At the appropriate time, he presented a poppy to each airman. As they were leaving the Aldergrove terminal building for their much needed rest, each airman wore a Remembrance Day poppy.

Meanwhile, back in Gander Airport, official arrival messages were received by the Gander radio operators, in turn, after each Hudson arrived at Aldergrove. The receipt of the seventh arrival message indicated that the mission of the night had been accomplished. The flight of the seven Hudsons had measured up to the highest expectations of all who were associated with the operation.

The sequel to the success of the flight of the seven Hudsons was the construction of Hangars 21 and 22 at Gander Airport. After completion, these hangars housed the Gander branch of the RAF Ferry Command. During the following five years, literally thousands of aircraft were delivered to the United Kingdom by the RAF Ferry Command from its Gander base.

In a 1992 Transport Canada volume of *History of Canadian Airports* by T.M. McGrath, it is recorded that 6,500 aircraft were delivered to the United Kingdom by the RAF Ferry Command from Gander Airport. In the overall operation, the losses sustained amounted to two per cent. In the same volume, it is also recorded that the United States Army Air Force delivered 10,000 aircraft over the North Atlantic from Gander Airport during the Second World War of 1939–1945.

The flight of the seven Hudsons may be seen to have come full circle at 3:30 p.m. on October 25, 1967, when Air Vice-Marshall Donald Clifford Tyndall Bennett, RAF (Retired), CB, CBE, DSO, returned to Gander to unveil the Atlantic Ferry Pilots Memorial on Burner Hill, in the environs of the Canadian Forces base.

In its original setting, the memorial took the form of a Lockheed Hudson, painted in wartime camouflage colours and mounted on a granite pedestal. The plaque which was attached to the pedestal was suitably engraved to mark the epic flight of the seven Hudsons and to commemorate not only the aviators who operated the first flight from Gander Airport but also the thousands of aviators and aircraft that followed them.

The Atlantic Ferry Memorial, which remained on Burner Hill for more than twenty years, was moved from its original setting in July 1990 for refurbishing. Subsequently, it was located on the town square of Gander during the summer months. It has found its permanent setting on the grounds of the new North Atlantic Museum, on the Trans-Canada Highway, near the entrance to the town of Gander.

Memorial plaque unveiled by Air Vice-Marshall D.C.T. Bennett on October 25, 1967.

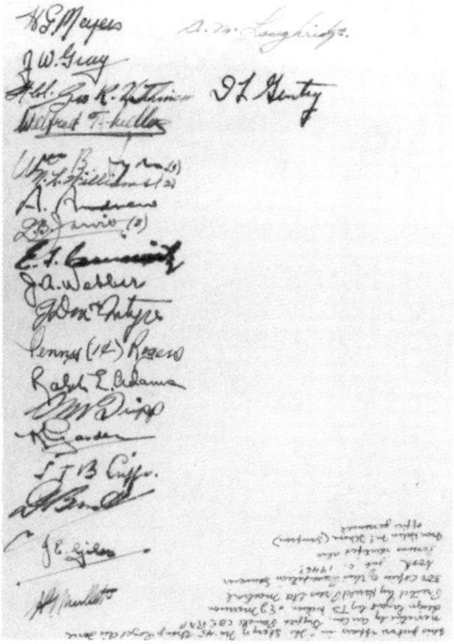

Shown above are the signatures of the twenty-two airmen who operated the flight of the seven Hudsons from Gander on November 10, 1940. (Photo by Griffith Powell. Department of National Defence, Canada, DND/CF Photo, PMR 85/476)

The Atlantic Ferry Pilot Memorial, Burner Hill, Gander. This memorial has since been moved from its original location, Burner Hill. It is now on the grounds of the Aviation Museum in Gander, on the south side of the Trans-Canada Highway, near the entrance to the town.

The Atlantic Ferry Memorial now occupies a suitable place of honour which is accessible to all Canadians and travellers from all parts of the world. Present and future aviation enthusiasts, as well as historians and students, are now able to view the memorial and to recall the fortitude of the valiant airmen who operated the daring flight of the seven Hudsons from Gander Airport on November 10, 1940.

GOING HOME FOR CHRISTMAS

STARTING BACK IN JUNE OF 1936 at Milepost 213, on the then Newfoundland Railway, the workers who carved out of the wilderness the runways of Gander International Airport always looked forward to going home for Christmas. It was only a train ride away to connect with the final road home.

The mindset was so pervasive among the workers that they even made a joke about it. If they made it to the heavenly gate and were waiting to be assigned quarters, St. Peter would probably say, "There is no point in assigning rooms to these guys because they all are going home for Christmas."

During World War II, the total number of military personnel and civilians at Gander numbered more than ten thousand. In the midst of Christmas celebrations, one could often observe that faraway look in their eyes which reflected the desire to be home for Christmas.

During the Golden Years, 1946 to 1960, when twelve international airlines operated through Gander on a regular basis, many young people were attracted to the town. Approximately 3,000 people lived in comfortable apartments and single quarters. But, perhaps because their quarters were converted military buildings, they did not consider their living quarters to be their permanent homes. So, during the Christmas celebrations there was an underlying desire to be home, a place outside Gander where their roots lay.

Confederation with Canada and the subsequent construction of a townsite elevated Gander to a desirable place to be at Christmas. The relationship between Gander and Christmas was reversed. While some of Gander's baby boomer generation remained there, many have moved to other parts of the world. In any case, going home for Christmas for them now means going home to Gander, that beautiful town of ten thousand people in the province of Newfoundland and Labrador.

SIR WINSTON CHURCHILL AT GANDER

IT WAS A CHILLY MORNING AT Gander on December 2, 1953. For the workers on the midnight to 8:00 a.m. shift in the old Hanger 22 air terminal, it was just an ordinary day – until about 6:00 a.m.

Around that time, word flashed among them that a British Overseas Airway Corporation (BOAC) aircraft with Sir Winston Churchill on board was about to land for a refuelling stop.

The then British Prime Minister was en route from London to Bermuda for a tri-party meeting there with Dwight Eisenhower, President of the United States, and Joseph Laniel, President of France.

In the pre-jet era of transatlantic commercial aviation, it was not unusual for VIPs of every nationality and from every walk of life to be seen among the passengers who disembarked and remained in the terminal during the refuelling of the aircraft.

It depended on individual preference, however, as to whether or not one would make any special effort to see those famous personages.

For example, avid admirers of glamorous and handsome movie stars might have no interest whatsoever in seeing the discoverer of the Salk vaccine.

But the name of Sir Winston Churchill had a special magic. Everybody on shift, including this writer, wanted to see, and hopefully to hear the voice of, the famous British statesman.

It was not surprising, therefore, that all workers who could possibly tear themselves away from their duties for a few minutes converged toward the BOAC aircraft after it came to a stop in the parking area.

Cleaners dropped their brooms, mechanics laid down their tools, cooks left their cooking, weather forecasters took a break, and flight dispatchers abandoned their offices to the noisy clatter of the teleprinters.

After the flight crew disembarked, it was learned that Sir Winston was still resting, and some doubt was expressed that he would make an appearance.

The Gander assembly was patient and well-behaved. They seemed to accept the opinion that it would be asking too much to expect the old gentleman to rise from his warm bed and brave the chilly air of Gander. After all, his destination was sunny Bermuda. And he had reached his seventy-ninth birthday two days earlier.

There were no shouts of "We want Winnie!" The considerate crowd were content to gaze in awe at the aircraft and await developments.

Their patience was rewarded.

On board the aircraft, Sir Winston, when he learned that there was a crowd outside, arose and emerged a few minutes later at the top of the aircraft ramp, dressed in a dark overcoat and a black homburg hat.

Sir Winston Churchill at Gander, December 2, 1953. L-R: Laurie Brown; Winston Churchill; George Watson.

As he held up his right hand in his famous "V" sign, the crowd cheered wildly. After the cheering subsided, Churchill wryly remarked, "You Newfoundlanders do rise at an early hour."

Sir Winston remained on the ramp long enough for a few camera-holders to take pictures. He then gracefully returned to his cabin.

Within a few minutes, the aircraft was winging its way to Bermuda.

It was a thrill for me to stand at the foot of the steps of the ramp to see Sir Winston Churchill and to catch him in the lens of my camera.

It was a greater thrill, however, to observe one of Sir Winston Churchill's outstanding characteristics, namely his great love of people, which motivated him to rise from his comfortable bed to greet a Gander crowd on that chilly morning of December 2, 1953.

A MEMORY OF DR. FREDERICK BANTING

A RECENT VISIT TO THE MEDICAL ward of the James Paton Memorial Hospital in Gander rang all the memory bells of my brief, but memorable, meeting with Sir Frederick Banting, the co-discoverer of insulin, first Canadian Nobel Prize winner, and a veteran of the two World Wars of the twentieth century.

Hanging on a wall near the nurses' station of the medical

ward is a large portrait of the famous Canadian doctor whom all sufferers of diabetes must sometimes silently thank for his leading role in the discovery of the drug that prolongs their lives.

In juxtaposition to the portrait is an impressive bronze plaque which marks the date September 12, 1941, when the then Royal Canadian Air Force hospital at Gander was dedicated to the memory of Banting by His Royal Highness The Duke of Kent. When the Banting hospital was replaced by the modern James Paton Memorial Hospital on May 15, 1964, both the portrait of Dr. Banting and the bronze plaque were hung in the new facility.

The 4:00 p.m. to midnight shift of February 19, 1941 in the Gander office of the Meteorological Service of Canada was a busy but quiet one for the two workers on duty, Hugh Bindon and myself.

Routinely, at that particular time – late evening – the office would be filled with flight crews of the RAF Ferry Command, who came for their final weather briefing on the North Atlantic and U.K. airports. But because of the prevailing Gander weather, all the flight crews were resting in their quarters at Eastbound Inn.

At about 10:00 p.m., the quiet of the weather office was disturbed by a gentle knock on the entrance door. When I responded to the knock, the man – who was dressed in the officer's uniform of the Canadian Army with the rank of major – identified himself with the words, "My name is Fred Banting."

He, too, was resting at Eastbound Inn and, before bedtime, decided to walk, unaccompanied, the 100 metres to the

Administration Building to visit the meteorological office on the third floor.

Although the building was guarded by Canadian Army soldiers, he was allowed admittance by the guards because of his rank and his reason for entrance to the building.

Because he was travelling as a passenger on one of the Hudson bombers on a special mission to England, Dr. Banting was interested in the weather picture over the North Atlantic and at the airports in the United Kingdom.

I introduced Dr. Banting to Hugh Bindon, the duty forecaster who, after completing his M.A. in Meteorology at the University of Toronto, had been stationed in Botwood during the flying boats era of the late 1930s. Bindon had also worked part-time in the Banting Institute at the University of Toronto during his student days there.

In fine professional style, which reflected his knowledge of North Atlantic weather, Bindon delivered a thorough, one-on-one briefing which pleased Dr. Banting and for which he expressed his thanks.

After an exchange of pleasantries in general conversation, Dr. Banting returned to his room in the Eastbound Inn. Hudson bomber T-9449, with crew members Captain Joseph Mackey, Navigator William Bird, Radio Operator William Snailham, and Dr. Frederick Banting as passenger, took off from Gander at 1958 GMT, February 20, 1941.

Less than an hour after takeoff, Snailham requested from the Gander radio operator a radio bearing for return to Gander, on account of engine trouble. Although the bearing was given promptly, it was never acknowledged and the aircraft crash landed near Musgrave Harbour.

Dr. Frederick Banting. (National Archives of Canada)

Captain Mackey was the only survivor of the crash landing. While Dr. Banting survived the crash impact and was given assistance by Mackey, two days later the rescue party found him dead, face down in the snow. Near him were his diaries and other documents that he carried with him on his painful exit from the aircraft. Thus ended the life of a great Canadian, at the early age of forty-nine years.

Regrettably, no high-profile memorial exists in Gander to honour Dr. Banting. Although the majority of Gander's streets are named for famous aviators – and there are exceptions in the naming of some streets – an exception was never made for Dr. Banting.

In my memory, Dr. Banting had an impressive presence because of his physical stature and his reputation worldwide as a medical scientist. However, in common with other great achievers whom I have met in my long life-time, he was unassuming and humble in general manner and demeanour.

In light of that memory, perhaps he would be quite content to be remembered in Gander by his portrait and the bronze plaque that may be seen only by visitors to the medical ward of the James Paton Memorial Hospital.

FLIGHT TO ROME

THE YEAR WAS 1952, ONE OF the peak years of Gander International Airport's golden age, when practically all the commercial aircraft flying between North America and Europe landed at Gander. During that period in global aviation, Gander was appropriately called the Crossroads of the World.

I was working at the Gander International Airport at that time as a FAA-certified flight dispatcher with Pan American World Airways. There was a FAA requirement that flight dispatchers – who computed the flight plans, briefed the captains, and maintained flight watch – make periodic familiarization flights over the scheduled routes.

This requirement, combined with a courtesy phone call and the luck of the Irish, led to a special audience with the Pope in Rome.

In March 1952, a few months after Pan Am extended its passenger service to Rome, my wife Alice and I boarded the flight after it arrived from New York for refuelling.

After we were settled away at a hotel near the Spanish

Steps, one of the city's best-known landmarks, I made a courtesy phone call to the Canadian College.

We were aware that Father Dermot O'Keefe, a student from St. John's, was doing post-doctoral studies in Rome and was a resident of the college. During our conversation, I casually inquired about the possibility of seeing the Pope during our visit.

During our sightseeing over the next few days – visiting such places as the Forum, the Colosseum, the Catacombs, and St. Peter's Basilica, and while mingling with the crowds on the Via Veneto – I completely forgot about my casual remark to Father O'Keefe.

It was a pleasant surprise, therefore, when I opened a sealed envelope which was handed to me one day when we returned to the hotel. The envelope contained a formal invitation to attend a special audience with the Pope.

The audience had been prearranged for a group of twenty Canadians who were visiting Rome. No doubt with some prompting from Father O'Keefe, Father Emile Boucher, the rector of the Canadian College, had managed to have two more Canadians included in the audience.

The meeting was scheduled for March 24, 1952. It was our last day in Rome, but there was ample time to attend the audience and catch the scheduled Pan Am flight leaving Rome that day.

As we travelled to the Vatican by bus, hundreds of university students wearing tall, cone-shaped hats poured out of the side streets, blocking the movement of all traffic. The students were carrying large placards which read, "Basso Tito" ("Down with Tito").

Guards on duty at Vatican City.

Left: The author with Father Dermot O'Keefe at St. Peter's Square, Rome. Right: The author with his wife, Alice (Curtis) Goff, RN at St. Peter's Square. Photos taken in March 1952.

At the time, the small state of Trieste, with a population of a little more than a quarter of a million, was under the administration of the United Nations but was being claimed by Tito of Yugoslavia, against the wishes of the people of Italy.

After getting off the bus and squeezing our way through the mob of students and finally hailing a taxi, we made it to the entrance of the papal chambers.

There, the Swiss Guard, in full regalia, scrutinized our invitation and promptly escorted us to the room where the other Canadians had already assembled.

Within a few minutes, after we formed an orderly semicircle, Eugenio Pacelli, Pope Pius XII, entered the room, accompanied by a cleric with the rank of Monsignor.

As he moved from person to person, speaking a few words to each one individually, he presented to each visitor a small packet, which contained a religious medal as a memento of the occasion.

Facing the assembly, he then moved to the centre of the room, imparted his blessing, and, with a final goodbye, gracefully exited the room.

The unplanned, unexpected, but definitely unforgettable special audience with Pope Pius XII had ended.

When Irish Eyes Were Smiling

When Irish eyes are smiling,
Sure it's like a morn in spring;

And when Irish eyes are smiling,
Sure they steal your heart away.

IRISH EYES WERE INDEED smiling at the passenger lounge of the Gander International Airport on the evening of October 26, 1983.

The date marked the twenty-fifth anniversary of the first jet flight across the North Atlantic by Pan American World Airways. A Boeing 707 aircraft, similar to the one used on the first Pan Am jet flight, made a fuel stop at Gander, as did the original flight.

In terms of progressively reduced landings, the introduction of long-range jet aircraft on the North Atlantic had a negative impact on Gander. Nevertheless, the then mayor, Doug Sheppard, and his councillors sponsored a twenty-fifth anniversary celebration while the aircraft was being refuelled and serviced.

Perhaps because of Pan Am's long and historic connection with Newfoundland, dating back to its Clipper flying boats through Botwood and including the thousands of propeller-driven aircraft through Gander in more recent years, Mayor Sheppard and the councillors must have decided that a modest celebration was appropriate for the occasion.

When the special Boeing 707 aircraft arrived at Gander from New York, Mayor Sheppard, the town councilors, and a number of invited guests had already gathered in the passenger lounge to greet the disembarking passengers and crew.

The passengers immediately caught the spirit of the celebration and mingled with the guests, many of whom were former employees of Pan Am, and other guests who had worked for the oil companies that serviced the aircraft used on the first Pan Am jet flight.

Among the passengers on the anniversary flight were many distinguished Americans who – in one way or another – had a connection with Pan Am, or with aviation in general.

Those who come readily to my mind are: Sam Miller, a retired chief pilot of Pan Am; Ed Trippe, son of Juan Trippe, the founder of Pan Am; Floyd Patterson, the well-known heavyweight boxing champion; and Maureen O'Hara, one of Ireland's famous movie stars and singers.

O'Hara's late husband, Charles F. Blair, had been a Pan Am captain on the North Atlantic routes.

My invitation to the celebration owed to the fact that I had entered the employ of Pan Am in April 1946. I received my airline training at the Pan Am School of Aviation at LaGuardia Airport in New York, and qualified for my Federal Aviation Administration (FAA) Flight Dispatcher's certificate on November 9, 1946.

I remained with the company until April 1961, when its dispatch function was terminated at Gander – another casualty of the introduction of long-range jet aircraft.

During the brief but pleasant social gathering, I was introduced to Maureen O'Hara as a person who had known Captain Charlie Blair when he flew through Gander. Indeed, I had computed his flight plan and briefed him many times. I was also aware of his services as a U.S. Navy pilot, as well as his daring solo flight on May 29, 1951, when he flew his converted military F-51 Mustang from Bardufoss, Norway over the North Pole to Fairbanks, Alaska.

The author with Maureen O'Hara at Gander Airport, October 26, 1983, the twenty-fifth anniversary of the first Pan Am jet flight through Gander across the North Atlantic.

I knew of the untimely death of Captain Blair – after his retirement – when he lost his life on takeoff while piloting his flying boat from the waters of the Virgin Islands on September 2, 1978.

Maureen O'Hara was obviously pleased to meet somebody in Gander who had known her husband and was eager to talk about him. During our conversation, she enlightened me on the circumstances of his death in the fatal crash of his flying boat.

The announcement of the departure of the twenty-fifth anniversary flight ended our discussion. But, as O'Hara prepared to join the other passengers who were boarding the aircraft for the continuation of the flight across the North Atlantic, I asked her for permission to take her picture. She pleasantly replied, "Why not have one taken with both of us together?"

I quickly passed my camera to Ed Pike of CBG Gander, who happened to be nearby covering the event for CBC. The resulting image captured the reality of the words of the song "When Irish Eyes Are Smiling." The luck of the Irish!

APRIL IN PORTUGAL

ONE OF THE POPULAR SONGS of the 1950s was "April in Portugal." It hit its peak in the spring of 1953 when it was interpreted by the band and chorus of Les Baxter.

The music of Raul Ferrao and the lyrics of Jimmy Kennedy tell of a short-lived romance in the intoxicating atmosphere of "April in Portugal," laced with music and wine.

In April 1951, with "April in Portugal" ringing in my ears almost daily on radio programs, I received a copy of *Vision of Fatima*, written in 1948 by Thomas McGlynn, a priest-sculptor. He relates his efforts to produce a faithful sculpture of the Blessed Virgin as she appeared to three children – Lucy, Jacinta, and Francisco – at Fatima, Portugal in 1917.

Because Lucy Dos Santos was still alive and a member of the Carmelite Order, Father McGlynn decided to travel to Portugal to seek her guidance in the production of his sculpture.

On his departure from New York, by commercial aircraft en route to Lisbon via Gander, he carried in a plywood box a small clay model of his proposed sculpture. To quote from his book:

> The box looked so much like a carpenter's tool kit and I looked so little like a carpenter that questions were soon asked. Over coffee at the gallery of the plane, at breakfast in the airport at Gander and in the cabin during the long, bright flight over the Atlantic, I had to tell many times the contents of the box, the reason for my trip and the story of Fatima.

In August 1977, about twenty-five years after I first heard "April in Portugal" and read *Vision of Fatima* my wife was terminally ill in the Wellesley Hospital, Toronto. When a friend who had just returned from Portugal presented her with a crucifix made of wood from a Fatima oak tree, she was overjoyed. For my part, the gift rang all the memory bells of "April in Portugal" and *Vision of Fatima.* After my wife's death

A section of Estoril Beach, Portugal, taken by the author in April 1980 from a high-level outdoor dining room of one of the many tourist hotels along Lisbon's famous beach.

in December 1978, I decided to visit Portugal, preferably in April.

"April in Portugal" became a reality for me in 1980. The TAP Portugal aircraft took off from Mirabel Airport on the afternoon of Easter Sunday, and arrived in Lisbon in the early morning of Easter Monday. Before nightfall, I was settled away in a hotel in Estoril. The bar at the hotel was cozy and friendly. The repertoire of the young piano player ranged from classical and semi-classical to the popular songs of our North American culture. Although "April in Portugal" had waned in popularity after thirty years, it was again ringing in my ears in the appropriate setting. I met a group of American and Canadian tourists and gladly accepted their invitation to join them on their bus journey to Fatima in the morning.

On April 10, 1980, I was at Fatima, and, to use a good Newfoundland expression, "I was taking it all in!" Mass at the Chapel of Apparitions, rosary outdoors, and mingling among the hundreds of people who were there from all parts of the world.

I fell into conversation with a retired U.S. naval officer who had gone to Fatima for a two-week vacation but was still there two years later acting as a volunteer tourist guide. When I mentioned my hope of seeing the completed sculpture of Father McGlynn, he led me to the foot of the steps of the Basilica.

"If you look down," he said, "you will notice the pavement stones here are well-worn and discoloured more than the others, because this is where Father McGlynn spent many days doing his sculpture."

He told me that Father McGlynn was dead and the book *Vision of Fatima* was a collector's item. Sister Lucy Dos Santos was still alive, and, from silver wire and mother-of-pearl, she had made the rosary which was in the right hand of the impressive white marble sculpture of the Blessed Virgin, which is visible to all who visit the Basilica.

At that moment, both the book *Vision of Fatima* and the song "April in Portugal" had come full circle for me.

GANDER MEMORIES OF J.R. SMALLWOOD

THE HONOURABLE JOSEPH Roberts Smallwood – who is frequently called the Last Father of Confederation – moved from St. John's, the capital city of Newfoundland and Labrador, in 1943. Although he was at that time a well-known journalist and radio broadcaster, he put his successful career in the media on hold and moved to Gander Airport in the central area of the island of Newfoundland. In 1943, Gander Airport was an important military base, not only for the Royal Canadian Air Force (RCAF), but also for the Canadian Army and the United States Army Air Force (USAAF). It was also an important base for the Royal Air Force Ferry Command, which was ferrying across the North Atlantic badly needed bombers to the United Kingdom.

During his residence in St. John's, Smallwood had kept a private farm on the outskirts of the city and raising pigs was a part of that modest farming venture. When the Commanding Officer of the Royal Air Force Ferry Command at Gander Airport invited J.R. Smallwood to manage a proposed piggery on the base, the man who would lead Newfoundland and Labrador into Confederation with Canada six years later readily accepted. The main purpose of the piggery was to provide a steady supply of pork for both the military and civilian personnel on the base and for the thousands of the aircrew who ferried the bombers across the North Atlantic to the United Kingdom.

The piggery was located in the environs of Hangars 21 and 22, the two that serviced the bombers at Gander and where the RAF Ferry Command headquarters were located. Living quarters for both the staff on the base and itinerant aircrew were also located in the general area, in buildings named Jupiter, Saturn, and Mars. But no matter where one worked, or whether one was a ground staff worker or an itinerant aircrew member, the gathering place for all at mealtime was the cafeteria.

As a member of the Gander office of the Meteorological Service of Canada, with its location in Hangar 21, my first meeting with J.R. Smallwood was in the cafeteria, where he mingled freely among the hundreds of both genders who ate there. On some occasions, he would be seated at a single table scanning newspapers and making notes while he was having his meal. In the later years of his political career, he revealed that he conceived the notion of bringing Newfoundland and Labrador into Confederation while he was a resident of Gander Airport. One would not be stretching the imagination too much if one concluded that his taking notes from newspapers were in some way related to his post–World War II plans for the Confederation movement.

Because Newfoundland and Labrador were ruled by a Commission of Government appointed by the British Government, there was absolutely no political activity that would have involved oratorical skills. During his stay at Gander Airport, however, an opportunity arose that enabled Smallwood to participate in group discussions on a variety of topics. Weekly discussion meetings in an open forum were organized by two Air Force Chaplains, one from the Royal Canadian Air Force, the other from the United States Army Air Force. No formal membership was required and the subject for discussion could be proposed by anyone in attendance. The meetings were held in a Quonset hut which was also used as a chapel by the United States Army Air Force. Because this was on the American side of the airport, J.R. Smallwood – who rarely, if ever, missed a meeting – joined the other passengers on the bus ride from the RAF Ferry Command base to attend. Although he played a prominent role in any discussion and initiated topics for discussion – in my memory, at least – he never did bring up a discussion on the pros and cons of Newfoundland and Labrador joining Canada after the end of World War II. With respect to these meetings, it is worthy of note that the American chaplain, a Jesuit priest, remarked in a private conversation after a meeting that J.R. Smallwood was evidently a well-informed and knowledgeable person on many subjects.

After the end of World War II in August 1945, the activities of the Royal Air Force Ferry Command were gradually phased out, as were those of the Royal Canadian Air Force, the Canadian Army, and the United States Army Air Force. Because the piggery had also served its purpose, it too was phased out. Nevertheless, J.R. Smallwood did not return to St. John's. The political situation in Newfoundland and Labrador was about to change. After ruling Newfoundland and Labrador for more than a decade – as what one might call a benevolent dictatorship – the Commission of Government was about to organize a National Convention. Delegates from various districts would be duly nominated and elected to the National Convention in order to decide on their future form of government for Newfoundland and Labrador.

Because Gander Airport was included in the district of Bonavista Centre, Smallwood decided to seek the nomination and election for that district. The nearby Town of Gambo – where he was born – was also included in the district of Bonavista Centre. As one would expect, he chose to be nominated in his birthplace on the nomination day of May 31, 1946.

On election day, June 21, 1946, J.R. Smallwood defeated his single opponent by a large majority. When the delegates met in St. John's on September 11, 1946, he was just another member of the National Convention whose delegates would spend about two years debating what would be the best form of government for the people of Newfoundland and Labrador. As a member of the National Convention, Smallwood emerged as a powerful pro-Confederate orator who would indeed lead Newfoundland and Labrador into Confederation on April 1, 1949.

During his campaign for his election as a member of the National Convention, Smallwood organized the Gander Co-operative Society, which is still a thriving business with a membership of approximately seven thousand people. There was a need for a grocery store in the new community of people who still remained in Gander and were employed by either the government or by the many commercial airlines. The modern Co-op store in the town of Gander today is a visible result of his initiative and reflects his concern for the welfare of others. In addition to the retail store, the Gander Co-op has a huge warehouse in the industrial section of the town which is the distributing centre to supply other Co-op stores on the island of Newfoundland.

My memory of J.R. Smallwood, in relation to the Gander Co-operative Society, is that, one day while walking with my wife, Alice, we met him and in casual conversation he asked us if we had joined the Co-op. When we replied in the negative, he replied, "Well, you should because it is meant to benefit young couples like you." Of course, we agreed and promptly headed for the Co-op store, where we took out membership for the modest sum of five dollars.

As the first premier of the new province of Newfoundland and Labrador and the person who held that position for twenty-three consecutive years, J.R. Smallwood wielded extensive political power and influence. Nevertheless, he did not cut himself off from his old Gander friends. On a visit with a friend to the old House of Assembly in St. John's to listen to the debates, we seated ourselves in the general seating section. We had hardly settled in our seats when we were approached by Smallwood, who escorted us to front-row seats. In the autumn of 1961, when Premier Smallwood was at the height of his career, I visited him in his office in the new

Confederation Building. Despite the fact that I had made no appointment in advance, when he was given my name he instructed his secretary to escort me to his office, where he greeted me warmly. My last contact with Premier Smallwood was on December 31, 1978. My wife Alice had passed away on December 30 and he must have learned of her death from the media on the following day. Again showing his compassion and concern for others, he phoned my home in Gander from his home on Roache's Line to express his sympathy. Premier Smallwood himself died on December 18, 1991, one week before he would have reached his ninety-first birthday.

In retrospect, there is always the question of whether Smallwood's surprising move from St. John's to Gander Airport was part of a long-range plan to bring Newfoundland and Labrador into Confederation with Canada or whether he made the move for other reasons. For example, he may have moved to assist in the war effort, even at the expense of interrupting his career as a journalist and radio broadcaster. His political insight, however, would have made him realize that there would be a change in the political structure of Newfoundland and Labrador after the end of World War II. The presence of both Canadian and American troops in St. John's, Stephenville, Argentia, Goose Bay, and Gander had a positive effect on the residents of those places, in that there was suddenly full employment available and knowledge gained of the way of life in Canada and in the United States. Indeed, when World War II ended, there was a movement in St. John's to have an economic union with the United States.

Another group of influential people in St. John's were strongly in favour of the restoration of Responsible

Government to Newfoundland and Labrador as the first step in any possible economic union with the United States or Confederation with Canada. The general opinion of that particular group was that bargaining from a position of Responsible Government would be stronger than from a delegation from the National Convention.

By remaining in the community of Gander, which was populated by young people with open minds on the form of government which would be the most beneficial for Newfoundland and Labrador, J.R. Smallwood experienced no formidable opposition to the Confederation movement. By living in Gander, he also had easy access to the many rural communities in the district of Bonavista Centre. In his hundreds of door-to-door visits to the homes in that district, he could explain in detail the many social benefits that would come to them immediately after Confederation with Canada – such as old-age security and monthly allowances for children and handicapped people. In a sense, it was a politician's dream situation, in that he could promise social benefits that would indeed come true under Confederation with Canada.

During the debates in the National Convention on the future possible forms of government, the three options were: retention of the Commission of Government; the restoration of Responsible Government; or Confederation with Canada. In the final referendum, in which Confederation with Canada was the choice of the majority of voters, there was no doubt that the voters in the rural districts were the people who tipped the scales in favour of it.

While Smallwood's surprise move from St. John's to Gander Airport in 1943 had all the appearances of a retrograde step in relation to his career as a journalist and radio broadcaster, from his Gander location he had time to think and to perceive the big picture of political change that was about to happen in Newfoundland and Labrador after the end of World War II. Because Responsible Government was the form of government during the early years of the Great Depression of the 1930s, J.R. Smallwood may have concluded that Responsible Government would not be the choice of the majority of voters. That form of government was associated with hard times. And while the Commission of Government was associated with the prosperity of the World War II years, there was no doubt that the residents of Newfoundland and Labrador desired to return to some form of democratic government.

In his wisdom, J.R. Smallwood put his media career behind him and entered the political arena as the ringleader of the Confederation movement, to the extent that he is remembered in history as the Last Father of Confederation.

THERE WAS NO SIGN OF THE PURPLE

IN MY GROWING UP, archbishops, deans, and monsignori always displayed very prominently their Roman Purple. As I remember, they wore great purple stocks under their Roman collars. Although I spent some of my boyhood years in a monsignor's parish and served the saintly gentleman for a few years as an altar boy, I was never very comfortable in the presence of the Roman Purple, almost to the point of having an aversion for it.

There was a stir of excitement in Gander on February 11, 1946. On that day, three Trans World Airlines (TWA) planes – *The Star of Vatican City, The Star of Rome,* and *The Colosseum* – landed in Gander. The three planes were carrying Archbishops Spellman, Mooney, Stritch, and Glenon, together with a number of other American bishops and monsignori. All were en route to Rome to attend a papal consistory at which the archbishops were to be elevated to the rank of Cardinal.

Although I was a great admirer of Archbishop Spellman, the distance between him and me that day was so great that I didn't get a good look, let alone speak to him or shake his hand. Meantime, a co-worker of mine in the Gander weather office, John Moakler, undeterred by the array of Roman Purple, moved in close with his camera. Knowing my admiration of Archbishop Spellman, John later gave me the picture.

Almost six years later, while working the graveyard shift as a flight dispatcher with Pan Am at Gander, I received an early-morning message from an aircraft that I was controlling. The aircraft was a westbound transatlantic flight heading to Boston but was making an unscheduled landing at Gander for fuel because of poor weather conditions at its final destination. Francis Cardinal Spellman was aboard, travelling alone, and the message relayed that he wished to say Mass in the airport chapel during the refuelling process. I called Father Phil McCarthy a few minutes later. As usual, "Father Mac" responded cheerfully and, within a short time, he was at the chapel and had it in readiness for the cardinal's arrival.

By the time the aircraft landed at Gander, I was off-duty and free to attend Cardinal Spellman's Mass. Father McCarthy assisted at the Mass and afterwards introduced to the cardinal the few airport employees who were in attendance. For my part, on that morning I happened to be carrying a small black book called a missal. If you are a reader under age thirty, you may not be familiar with the old custom of each person keeping his or her own missal instead of picking one up in church. Today, the little black book bears the inscription, "Roderick Goff, with a blessing, Francis Cardinal Spellman, Gander, Newfoundland, January 20, 1952."

Then Archbishop (later Cardinal) Francis Spellman at Gander Airport on February 11, 1946, en route to Rome to receive his higher rank.

As an afterthought, you may wonder how I managed to cope with such a close encounter with the Roman Purple. Well, it was like this. Cardinal Spellman was returning from his Christmas visit with the American troops in Korea. As Military Vicar, he was wearing the appropriate U.S. Army uniform, topped by an army parka, which extended almost to his ankles. There was no sign of the purple! It is no wonder, then, that when my turn came to be introduced by Father McCarthy, I felt comfortable enough to ask the cardinal to autograph my missal!

MEMORIES OF THE USAAF WEATHER UNIT

ALTHOUGH THE OPERATIONS of the United States Army Air Force (USAAF) at Gander Airport during World War II have been well-documented by military historians and aviation writers, the memories of this writer are concerned mainly with the members of the weather unit of the USAAF troops who came to Gander in the summer of 1941.

The USAAF weather unit was under the control of Captain Clark L. Hosmer, a graduate of West Point, the famous American military academy. Captain Hosmer was also a qualified B-17 bomber pilot. He was, in time, promoted to the rank of Colonel.

When the members of the USAAF weather unit arrived at Gander, they were invited by Patrick D. McTaggart-Cowan – the meteorologist in charge of the Canadian weather office – to share the facilities and space of the Canadian office on the third floor of the Administration Building. The weathermen of the USAAF performed their duties there for many months while they waited for their own office to be ready. They were there on December 7, 1941, when Pearl Harbor was attacked by Japanese aircraft. Their presence in the Canadian weather office at that date is memorable for this author because, after the attack became known, one of the USAAF weathermen informed us that he had a brother serving in the Pacific and he had some anxiety for his safety.

A member of the USAAF weather unit plotting the wind run.

A newsletter was issued periodically by the USAAF weather unit at Gander. The following quotes are taken from the Winter 1945 issue:

> 1."Particular credit can be given to Lt. Col. Clark L. Hosmer, Majors Lynn T. Irish and Robert M. Rados and Captain Russell Roberts whose perseverance and energy during pioneer days enable this weather station to become one of the finest in the region."

2."Weather personnel have been responsible for the participation in many memorable occasions at their base. When the American flag was first raised over Gander on August 8, 1941, weather personnel were present to honour the flag. The operation of the weather station caused great concern on December 21, 1941, when a field alert was called as a result of someone spotting a lantern suspended from a pibal balloon. After the lighted balloon had been released, it was hovering overhead in the field area, and no one was able to hear the plane's motor or to get a reply when challenged by the radio station. It was only after everyone was called outside in the dark snowy weather, and all street lights and field beacons shot out with 45s that the weatherman's balloon was discovered to be the cause of all the alarm and discomfort."

3."In spite of the long hours of the detailed nerve-racking eye-straining work of the weathermen 24 hours a day around the clock on Sundays and holidays (yes, the weather station operates on Christmas too) the weathermen have proved that their interest is not confined to surface, upper-air, isotropic, and adiabatic charts, to enciphering and deciphering weather data, making hydrogen to fill and release balloons for ceiling and wind data, to observe weather and try to forecast what is going to happen here and elsewhere, and all the one hundred and one worries of the weather-worry bird. The champion softball team of the 1944 season was none other than the hot rock forecasters. The 1943 forecasters basketball team won second place in the local league to be taken only by their archrivals, the AACS wavelengths."

A member of the USAAF weather unit waiting for release of the pilot balloon before measuring the upper wind.

ST. MARY'S BASILICIA, SYDNEY, AUSTRALIA

ON A VISIT TO SYDNEY, Australia in May 1993, it was my privilege to visit St. Mary's Basilicia in that city. With pardonable pride, the Australians claim that St. Mary's is the largest cathedral in the southern hemisphere and the eighth-largest cathedral in the world. Situated as it is in the centre of Sydney, adjacent to Hyde Park, it is almost impossible to miss. It is difficult for the amateur photographer to get a satisfactory picture of the huge structure from ground level. The best pictures of St. Mary's are taken from the top level of the nearby Sydney Tower, which rises to one thousand feet above the ground. Unfortunately, when I reached the level of the tower, I realized that, because my camera was not equipped with a telescopic lens, my pictures would not turn out as sharp as I would have desired.

My first visit to St. Mary's was a casual drop-in. While taking a sightseeing walk around the centre of the city, St. Mary's suddenly loomed before me in all its grandeur and majesty. After I climbed the steep stone steps and entered the cathedral, it was evident that a May Day procession was in progress. The cathedral was filled with people. Adults and children alike were participating in traditional May devotions to Mary, the Mother of Jesus, to whom the cathedral is dedicated.

On the following Sunday, I attended the 10:30 a.m. Eucharistic Celebration in St. Mary's. On entering the cathedral, all worshipers were given a leaflet which announced that it was the sixteenth of May, 1993, World Communication Day, and that the twenty-fifth Annual Media Mass would be celebrated, marking twenty-five years of the relationship between the church and the media. The celebrant of the Mass was Cardinal Edward Clancy, the con-celebrants Bishop John Heaps and many priests of the archdiocese of Sydney.

The Eucharistic Celebration was enhanced by a rich liturgy which included a Cathedral Choir of seventy men's and boys' voices and two cathedral organs. Because each organ is inadequate on its own, on account of the immenseness of the cathedral they are played simultaneously by two organists who keep in time with the aid of two-way headphones.

After the distribution of Holy Communion and the final blessing, Cardinal Clancy presented the archbishops of Sydney citations for media work during the past year. Separate awards were given to outstanding journalists in the press, radio, and television. These annual awards are not confined to Catholic journalists but are open to any and all members of the Australian media. After each person received his or her award, an enthusiastic round of applause was given by the congregation. The biggest ovation was given to a lady journalist who walked up to receive her award while holding the hand of her preschool-age daughter.

When a tour of the entire cathedral was offered to people who were interested, I joined a group of tourists who were anxious to accept the privilege. In the course of an hour, Father Vince Redden, the youthful-looking dean of the cathedral, escorted the group and in fine professional style related the rich history of St. Mary's. His interpretation of the sacred artworks and the thirty-nine stained glass windows was of special interest. Two of the windows, which are called the Rose Windows, are deserving of special mention. The one over the west entrance features Adam in the centre surrounded by Moses and other well-known prophets of the Old Testament. Its counterpart over the east entrance features

Christ, the Teacher, in the centre, surrounded by St. Paul and the four evangelists, Matthew, Mark, Luke, and John. The outer circle of the window includes John the Baptist and eleven Apostles. Symbolically, the message that the promises of the Old Testament are fulfilled in the New Testament is conveyed each day when the sun shines on the west window at sunset and rises the next day to shine on the east window.

Of special interest to me was the sculpture *La Pieta*, a replica in Carrara marble of Michelangelo's famous original, which may be seen by visitors to St. Peter's Basilica in Rome. I had seen the original *La Pieta* in March 1952, when I was accompanied by my now deceased wife. As a consequence, seeing the replica in St. Mary's rang a lot of bells for me. The *La Pieta* in St. Mary's is one of four similar replicas in the world and the only one outside of Italy. It was donated to St. Mary's in 1971 by David Jones Ltd. to mark the sesquicentenary of St. Mary's. Dean Redden pointed out that only the original *La Pieta* in St. Peter's has the signature of Michelangelo. It was

The author at the La Pieta *sculpture, St. Mary's Basilica, Sydney, Australia.*

inscribed by the famous sculptor on the veil of the Blessed Virgin.

No cathedral the size of St. Mary's would be complete without bells. The Bells of St. Mary's Basilica consist of a peal of fourteen bells which were cast at the Whitechapel foundry in England. They were installed in the central tower in June 1986, replacing the previous eight which had been installed in 1882. The tenor bell from the original eight bells is displayed near the stairs leading to the crypt in the basement. The St. Mary's Basilica Society of Change Ringers ring the bells every Sunday and on special occasions.

The last point of interest on the tour was a visit to the crypt. Since 1946, the archbishops of Sydney, as well as Bishop Charles Davis and the pioneer priests Fathers John Therry, Daniel Power, and John McEnroe, lie entombed in the crypt. The story of Creation and the titles of Mary are depicted in the crypt's famous terrazzo mosaic floor. Conceptually, it was the work of the Catholic Biblical scholar, Monsignor William Leonard. The design was inspired in part by the Book of Kells and was executed over a period of fifteen years by the Melocco Brothers.

The history of St. Mary's Basilica is closely tied to the history of modern Australia. Of the six Australian states, New South Wales is the oldest. Its capital, Sydney, has a population of about three million at the present time. Founded as a penal station by the British Government in 1788, the first British governors at Sydney were naval and military officers in command of the garrison, the convicts, and a few free settlers. Many of the prisoners were militant Irish Catholics and included some Catholic priests. Under the harsh anti-Catholic

British penal laws of the eighteenth century, many of the prisoners were labelled as convicts and banished to Australia after being condemned without trial. The Irish ballad "The Fields of Athenry" tells that sad story.

One of the stained glass windows in the cathedral commemorates the celebration of the first Mass in Sydney by a convict priest, Father James Dixon, in 1803. The first two Catholic chaplains, Fathers John Therry and Philip Connolly, arrived in Sydney in 1820. The foundation of the first St. Mary's, then called a chapel, was laid in 1821 by the then British Governor Macquaire. On the evening of June 29, 1865, the first St. Mary's was destroyed by fire. On December 8, 1868, Archbishop Polding blessed the foundation of the present St. Mary's. The present structure, which was formally opened on September 8, 1882 by Archbishop Roger Vaughan, was built in various stages by a succession of bishops and archbishops of the diocese.

Down through the years, St. Mary's Basilica in Sydney has been the subject of many praiseworthy comments, not only from church leaders but also from political leaders. During my visit to Australia, I purchased a book of pen drawings of St. Mary's by Allan Gamble, a Fellow of the Royal Australian Institute of Architects. In the foreword of this book. A.E. Cahill, a Senior Lecturer of the University of Sydney, recalls some comments which are worthy of repetition in this piece.

In September 1928, when the cathedral was being made ready for the twenty-ninth International Eucharistic Congress, Premier Bavin of Australia, the son of a Methodist minister, drew a contrast between the surrounding "material" buildings and the "spiritual" cathedral when he stated, "It stands as a sermon in stone, a silent but eloquent witness to the truth that men do not live by bread alone." A.E. Cahill also recalls that Archbishop Roger Vaughan, the second archbishop of Sydney, frequently used the metaphor of the stones that "speak" when he was referring to St. Mary's. When he formally opened the cathedral on September 8, 1882, he predicted that St. Mary's "would speak to later generations of the faith of a generation that built it." More than a century later, A.E. Cahill reinforces the comments of Archbishop Vaughan when he himself writes, "It still speaks eloquently to those who will take the trouble to listen." Indeed, the St. Mary's Basilica of Sydney, Australia spoke eloquently to this visitor from Gander, Newfoundland, when he was privileged to make a May visit to this famous cathedral, to observe its beauty, to walk through its vast interior, to attend there a Eucharistic Celebration, and, what was equally important, to listen.

THE SPIRIT OF CHRISTMAS IN HANGAR 22

WHEN COMMERCIAL TRANSATLANTIC aviation began using Gander International Airport after the end of World War II, the spacious passenger lounge of the former RAF Hangar 22 was noted for the spirit of Christmas that was felt by all who visited there during the festive season.

In preparation for Christmas, Jack James, the then operations manager of the airport, always ensured that the tallest and most beautiful Christmas tree in the area of the airport was cut down and erected in a conspicuous place in the passenger lounge of the airport. During the Twelve Days of Christmas, the giant tree would be ablaze with lights and suitably decorated. Likewise, the gift shop and the ticket counters of airlines would all dress up in Christmas style. The almost perfect Christmas setting was made perfect by the Christmas music coming from the public address system.

During the Christmas holidays, the passenger lounge was visited, not only by Gander children and their parents, but also by the thousands of airline passengers of various nationalities who waited in the passenger lounge for an hour or more while their aircraft were being refuelled and serviced.

When it was necessary for the passengers to remain overnight, they were accommodated in three nearby buildings named Jupiter, Saturn, and Mars. If their delay was only a few hours, the passengers could dine in the dining room of the lounge where a bar named the Big Dipper was also located.

With so much Christmas spirit emanating from the passenger lounge of Hangar 22, and with three planets, Jupiter, Saturn, and Mars, and a cluster of stars, the Big Dipper, honoured there, how could Santa possibly overfly Gander Airport on Christmas Eve?

To the delight of the Gander children who might have had anxiety about Santa's arrival, they always realized when they awoke on Christmas morning that, regardless of weather conditions, Santa, with his bag of gifts and led by Rudolph the Red-Nosed Reindeer, had indeed made a safe landing at Gander Airport. The proof was in the gifts they found under their own Christmas trees and the cookies they had left for Santa vanished from the cookie dish.

MEMORIES OF THE ROYAL CANADIAN AIR FORCE

THE FIRST SQUADRON OF THE Royal Canadian Air Force (RCAF) flew their Digby aircraft into Gander Airport in the spring of 1940 to start anti-submarine patrols over the North Atlantic. Because their barracks and dining quarters were not ready, the pilots were accommodated in the Administration Building, where the civilian radio operators, the staff of the meteorological office, and the administrative staff were quartered. All the occupants of the building were served their meals in the spacious dining room on the first floor, where movies were shown frequently in the evenings.

The pilots of the Digby aircraft were those who had been trained in peacetime when the minimum educational level for RCAF pilot training was two years' university. In fact, the group included university graduates in various studies. The pilots were accompanied by a young doctor who had enlisted in the RCAF after graduating from university in 1940.

By 1941, the RCAF hospital was built and fully staffed by RCAF doctors, nurses, and other medical personnel. A separate dental clinic was part of the hospital site. It is worthy of note that, when Dr. Frederick Banting was delayed at Gander for three days in February 1941, he made a special visit to the hospital to show his concern for the patients there. Unfortunately, Dr. Banting lost his life on February 21, 1941, when the Hudson aircraft in which he was flying to the United Kingdom crashed near Musgrave Harbour. Responding to the proposal of the RCAF doctors, on September 12, 1942 the visiting Duke of Kent named the hospital the Banting Memorial Hospital.

The first operations centre of the RCAF was a room on the third floor of the Administration Building, near the meteorological office. In due course, the permanent oprations centre was located in an underground structure on the Canadian Army side of Gander. The anti-submarine operation was expanded by the addition of long-range Canso aircraft, Hudsons, and B-24 Liberators. Members of the Women's Division of the RCAF ("WDs") as well as male officers provided around-the-clock flight watch and air traffic control to the RCAF aircraft in flight. In order to provide immediate weather information when it was required, a civilian weather forecaster and a civilian meteorological technician were also on duty at all times in the underground operations centre.

The huge RCAF recreation centre included a swimming pool and facilities for various other athletics such as basket-

Canada's Snowbirds over Gander, NL in the summer of 1980.

ball, badminton, and boxing. The centre was a hive of activity daily because members of the armed forces and civilians were welcome to use the facilities at will. During the winter, one could sign out a ski outfit at the centre if one wished to spend a few hours on the Gremlin ski trail near Gander Lake.

The RCAF also had a superb brass band which made its appearance on appropriate occasions, such as parades, concerts, and when dances were held in the recreational centre.

On January 1, 1944, the RCAF established the first radio station in Gander in the basement of the home of the commanding officer, Group Captain Clare Annis. It was operated daily by the members of the RCAF under the name of VORG, the Voice of Radio Gander. In the postwar years, it was taken over by the Newfoundland Broadcasting Company. When Newfoundland and Labrador became a province of Canada on April 1, 1949, it came under the management of the Canadian Broadcasting Corporation and was named CBG. Shortly after the start of the construction of a Gander townsite in 1952, CBC selected a site for radio station CBG in a solid brick building on Sullivan Avenue. Because CBG has its roots in the Gander operations of the RCAF in World War II, it has great historical value to the residents of Gander.

MEDICAL SERVICES AT GANDER, 1936–2005

DURING THE CONSTRUCTION period of Gander Airport between June 1936 and November 1938, Dr. Arthur

Knapp, the resident doctor of Lewisporte, made periodic visits to what was then called Milepost 213. The site was so termed because of its distance from St. John's on the trans-insular railway that, at that time, operated between St. John's and Port aux Basques. After the airport was ready to receive aircraft in the autumn of 1938, Dr. Knapp continued to visit Gander to hold a clinic in the Administration Building.

After World War II broke out in September 1939, and the Royal Canadian Air Force (RCAF) came to Gander in the spring of 1940, an RCAF hospital was constructed and was ready in 1941. Because the RCAF hospital was fully staffed with their own doctors, nurses, and other support staff, there was no need for Dr. Knapp to continue his visits to Gander. An RCAF dental clinic in a separate building near the main entrance to their hospital was also ready to receive patients. The services at both the hospital and the dental clinic were available, not only to the members of the RCAF, but also to the members of the regiments of the Royal Canadian Army, the Royal Air Force Ferry Command, and to civilians who were employed at Gander.

On September 12, 1942, the RCAF hospital was officially named the Banting Memorial Hospital by the visiting Duke of Kent. During Dr. Banting's three-day delay at Gander, on account of unfavourable flying weather, he visited the RCAF hospital and showed concern for the patients there. Dr. Banting lost his life after the Hudson Bomber on which he was flying as a passenger took off from Gander on February 20, 1941, en route to the United Kingdom, and crashed near Musgrave Harbour. The original sixty-five-bed Banting Memorial Hospital was later enlarged to 100 beds.

On April 1, 1946, the Banting Memorial Hospital was taken over by the Department of Health of the Government of Newfoundland and Labrador. On that day, the only doctor on duty was James Paton and the only registered nurse on duty my late wife, Alice Curtis Goff, a graduate of the 1942 class of St. Clare's Mercy Hospital. Within a few months, additional doctors, registered nurses, and other support staff were employed at the hospital. Eli Baker, a former high-school teacher, was appointed business manager. After the death of Dr. James Paton in February 1962, Dr. Melvin Coxon was appointed to the position of Director of Medical Services.

In common with all the buildings that were used during World War II, the Banting Memorial Hospital was deteriorating and had to be replaced by a permanent building. A new hospital was constructed on the south side of the Trans-Canada Highway, near the entrance to the town of Gander. It was formally opened on May 25, 1964 and was named the James Paton Memorial Hospital. Dr. Melvin Coxon remained Director of Medical Services until his retirement in September 1978. Dr. Ted Shapter, who succeeded Dr. Coxon, remained until August 31, 1989, when he returned to St. John's. After Dr. Shapter's departure, Dr. Peter Blackie was appointed Director of Medical Services.

During the year 2005, retirement came to three persons who each had a long and distinguished career at the James Paton Memorial Hospital and on the Central East Health Care Board. Chief Executive Officer (CEO) David Lewis retired on April 7, 2005. His service began in 1974 after his graduation from the University of Toronto with a degree in hospital administration. The associate CEO, Elizabeth Forward, retired after thirty-five years of unbroken service. Starting as a registered nurse, she was promoted to various supervisory positions, including Director of Nursing, on her way to a top management position. Dr. Peter Blackie, who grew up in Gander, returned to his hometown after his graduation from Dalhousie University and spent his entire medical career in Gander.

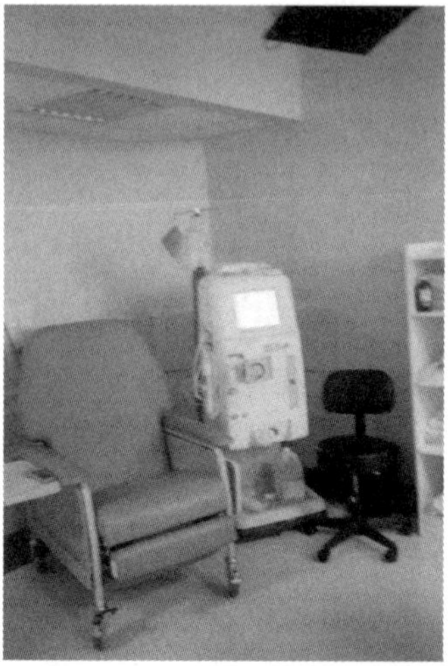

One of the renal dialysis units at the Renal Dialysis Centre of the James Paton Memorial Hospital, Gander, NL. Photo taken by author in February 2005.

Down through the years, the James Paton Memorial Hospital has expanded, not only by extensions to the original building, but also by increasing the medical staff in order to cope with the medical needs of the ten thousand residents of Gander and similar needs of the residents of the neighbouring towns, such as Glenwood, Gander Bay, Carmanville, Musgrave Harbour, Wesleyville, and Gambo. The latest addition to the James Paton Memorial Hospital is a state-of-the-art Renal Dialysis Centre, which has eight units for patients.

The new dialysis centre received its first patient on February 28, 2005 and was formally opened on March 29, 2005 by the Honourable Kevin O'Brien, MHA for Gander. Before the end of the year 2005, a new enlarged cancer clinic will be completed at the James Paton Memorial Hospital.

In addition to the medical services given at the James Paton Memorial Hospital, eleven doctors have their clinics in the Gander Medical Building. Public health nurses who serve the Gander area have their offices in the Blundon Building.

It may be observed that, from the first visits of Dr. Knapp in 1936 until the present time, in both war and peace, medical services at Gander have kept pace with the aviation activities at the airport and with the ongoing increase in the population of Gander and its neighbouring towns.

A BIRD'S-EYE VIEW OF CANADA

IT WAS ON SUNDAY, MARCH 25, 1974 that a group of twenty-two people, employees and close relatives of employees of Eastern Provincial Airways, boarded one of the company's Boeing 737 jet aircraft for a flight from Gander to Vancouver. The flight was not a scheduled commercial one that was open to the general public. Because it was being ferried to Vancouver for technical purposes, revenue passengers were not permitted on the aircraft.

The pre-flight weather briefing indicated it was an unusually fine day from one end of Canada to the other.

High-pressure cells dominated the meteorological pattern to the extent that the forecast promised we would have visual contact with the ground along the entire route. All passengers, including this author, saw the journey as a privileged opportunity to get a "bird's-eye view" of the ten provinces of Canada.

Despite the unlikelihood of a hijacker being among us, we went through the normal airport security process prior to boarding the aircraft.

Shortly after getting airborne, at 6:00 a.m. Gander time, we were advised by the captain that we would be making refuelling stops at both Montreal and Winnipeg and that we would be flying at a cruising altitude of 35,000 feet on each of the three legs of the flight to Vancouver.

The official flight plans, computed on the basis of the known performance of the aircraft, as well as the prevailing winds and temperatures, indicated that our flight time to Montreal would be two and a half hours, Montreal to Winnipeg, three hours, and the final leg, Winnipeg to Vancouver, two hours and forty-five minutes.

We were aware that we would be passing through five time zones en route to Vancouver and that we had the choice of setting back our watches progressively as we passed through each, or of making a single adjustment of four and a half hours after we arrived at Vancouver.

A cursory check of the passengers on board showed that almost every department of the company was represented in the group. In addition to the captain and the first officer, we spotted a third off-duty pilot, two aircraft engineers, and a radio technician. Three well-behaved preschool children and an elderly couple provided the final touch to create a homely atmosphere of good companionship.

Passing through the first time zone, the unique half-hour Newfoundland time zone, our course took us a little south of Stephenville. Before we could get a good look at the former United States Army Air Force buildings and the new Linerboard Mill, our attention was drawn to the north shore of Nova Scotia. A few minutes later, we were looking down on the peaceful farms of Prince Edward Island.

In the second time zone, we passed directly over the elm-treed city of Fredericton, New Brunswick, which happened to be the home-town of the captain of our aircraft. We felt that he must have been longing to make the fuel stop at his home-town airport instead of Montreal, but the fuel gauges dictated otherwise.

After catching a fleeting glimpse of Sherbrooke and the eastern townships of Quebec, we landed at Montreal's Dorval airport. It was 7:00 a.m. Montreal time, 8:30 a.m. back in Gander. We had flown two and a half hours, moving west-ward with the apparent westward movement of the sun. True, we were not moving as fast as the sun, but we were indeed moving at jet aircraft speeds.

After the half-hour fuel stop at Montreal, we were air-borne for Winnipeg. As we passed over Ottawa to the nickel mining city of Sudbury, and on to Winnipeg via Lake Superior and Thunder Bay, the friendly spirit of the group came to the fore. Even though no special in-flight services were expected, box lunches and refreshments suddenly appeared on the scene. The aircraft engineer proved to be an excellent brewer of coffee, while the off-duty pilot could serve a tray of sandwiches with the skill and aplomb of an experienced waiter. On the descent into Winnipeg, we had an excellent view of some of the spacious farmlands of Manitoba. Touchdown was made at 9:30 a.m. Winnipeg time. It was noon back in Gander.

Under the blue sky of Winnipeg, the aircraft was refuelled for the final leg to Vancouver. For those of us on board who had never visited Western Canada, the last leg of our journey proved to be the most impressive one. As we moved from Manitoba to Saskatchewan, miles and miles of unbelievably flat prairie country passed beneath us. The weather held as good as promised in the forecast. Off to the left we could see clearly the city of Regina lying neatly in the middle of farming country.

Moving from Saskatchewan to Alberta via Medicine Hat and on to British Columbia via Cranbrook, Princeton, and Hope, we were privileged to see the famed Canadian Rockies at their best. The brilliant sun shining on the majestic snow-capped peaks was perhaps the most awesome sight of the entire journey. Those among us who had cameras used them to capture the impressive sight, while others continued to stare in silence.

In due time, the lush, green countryside appearing beneath the aircraft indicated that we were approaching Vancouver. A few minutes later, the city appeared in full view with the popular ski resort, Grouse Mountain, in the background. A safe and uneventful landing was made at 10:45 a.m. Vancouver time. It was 3:15 p.m. back in Gander.

As we stepped from the aircraft to enter the passenger arrival lounge at Vancouver airport, we could muse on the seeming contradiction in reference to time. While the actual elapsed time of our journey amounted to nine hours and fifteen minutes, our watches indicated that the difference between the Gander departure time and the Vancouver time was only four hours and forty-five minutes.

Thanks to the cloudless sky all across Canada, we had indeed realized our expectations of having a bird's-eye view of a significant part of each of the ten provinces of Canada. Verily, it was an object lesson in Canadian geography, a lesson which gave us a lasting appreciation of both the grandeur and the greatness of our native land, Canada.

Roderick B. Goff was born in Sydney, NS in 1916, the second son of John J. Goff and Annie (McNeil) Goff. He received his early education from the Sisters of the Congregation of Notre Dame and was an honours high-school graduate from the now defunct St. Patrick's Academy in Carbonear, NL.

His more than forty years in aviation operations at Gander Airport began in 1940 in the Gander office of the Meteorological Service of Canada. After he entered the employ of Pan American Airway in 1946, he received training at the company's aviation school at LaGuardia Airport in New York and received his Federal Aeronautics Authority Flight Dispatcher's licence on November 9, 1946. After fifteen years with Pan Am, he was employed by Eastern Provincial Airlines until his retirement in August 1981.

After his retirement from a technical career in aviation, Goff chose to return to university studies in the Humanities at Memorial University, St. Paul University, and the University of Ottawa, from which he received an honours cum laude degree in June 1991 – his third university degree.

He was married to the late Alice (Curtis) Goff, RN and has two sons and eight grandchildren. He lives in the airport town of Gander, NL.